Site Relia Engineering (SRE) Handbook

How SRE Implements DevOps

2

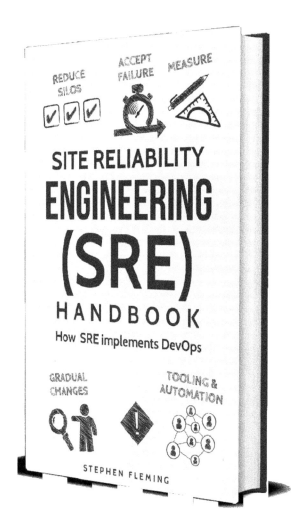

4

List of my Other Books

Technology

- [DevOps Handbook](#)
- [Microservices Architecture Handbook](#)
- [Blockchain Technology](#)
- [DevOps and Microservices](#)
- [Blockchain with DevOps & Microservices](#)
- [Kubernetes Handbook](#)

Mind and body

- [Love Yourself](#)
- [Intermittent Fasting](#)

6

Contents

BONUS TECHNOLOGY BOOKLET

Dear Friend,
I am privileged to have you onboard. You have shown faith in me and I would like to reciprocate it by offering the maximum value with an amazing booklet which contains latest technology updates on DevOps and Blockchain.

"Get Instant Access to Free Booklet and Future Updates"

- Link: http://eepurl.com/dge23r

OR

- QR Code : You can download a QR code reader app on your mobile and open the link:

Preface

Well, you have been hearing a lot about DevOps lately, wait until you meet a Site Reliability Engineer!

Google is the pioneer in the SRE movement and Ben Treynor from Google defines SRE as," "what happens when a software engineer is tasked with what used to be called operations". The ongoing struggles between Development and Ops team for software releases have been sorted out by mathematical formula for green or red-light launches!

Sounds interesting, now do you know which the organizations are using SRE: Apart from Google, you can find SRE job postings from: LinkedIn, Twitter, Uber, Oracle, Twitter and many more.

I also enquired about the average salary of a SRE in USA and all the leading sites gave similar results around $130,000 per year. Also, currently the most sought job titles in tech domain are DevOps & Site Reliability Engineer.

So do you want to know, How SRE

works, what are the skill sets required, How a software engineer can transit to SRE role, How LinkedIn used SRE to smoothen the deployment process.

Here is your chance to dive into the SRE role and know what it takes to be and implement best SRE practices.

The DevOps, Continuous Delivery and SRE movements are here to stay and grow, its time you to ride the wave!

So, don't wait and take action!

1. SRE Introduction

Intro

The main function of SRE is that the system's software, hardware, and firmware will perform its tasks satisfactorily. The task being the one for which the system was designed and created. This too within a stipulated time and in a specific environment.

SRE is an engineering discipline that includes certain aspects of software engineering to tackle IT operations related issues. The main objective is the creation of ultra-scalable and extremely reliable software systems. System engineering is the parent discipline of SRE or reliability engineering. SRE emphasizes the reliability factor in the product management lifecycle. Reliability or dependability is described as the capability of a system or its components to function normally in an understated condition for a stipulated period.

The main role of a reliability engineer is

to identify and manage risks involved in assets management. These risks could adversely affect business or workshop operations. This is a broad, primary role and can be divided into three smaller and more manageable roles such as loss estimation, LCAM (Life Cycle Asset Management), and risk management.

The main difference between DevOps and SRE's is DevOps' primary focus on coding and the kind of atmosphere you are in. DevOps are at the top of the pyramid in terms of software development. They are responsible for both architecture and system culture. They deliver tasks or develop infrastructure within the development process.

The Emergence of SRE (Site Reliability Engineer)

This branch of engineering has a developing importance in IT Operations. You can find more than a thousand listed on LinkedIn alone for this requirement. Although this job continues to gain importance, there is still a lot of confusion about the requirements. The SRE 2018 report has shown that the SRE role is evolving. There are many engineers who are happy in their organization but, at the same time, are struggling to explain their roles in the company. Another interesting fact highlighted in the survey was that SREs are present in all sizes of company and they hail from a range of backgrounds. It is not necessary that an ideal SRE is a generalist.

The SRE's role was first established by Google in 2003 while trying to cope up with its fast-growing production needs. Since then, several other companies have implemented SREs in their teams. Over the years the portfolio has increased with a requirement of software development and IT operational skills combined together. An SRE is expected to cover both areas of expertise.

The growth of SRE was pretty much expected, especially in the area of complex infrastructure where constant availability and speed is of paramount significance. As Google pointed out the SRE is a single point of arbiter and responsibility between Devs and Ops teams. They ensure reliable and low latency apps delivery.

SRE is a specialized job and focuses on maintainability and reliability of large environments. SREs couple operational responsibility with the competence of software engineering to navigate system architecture. They are expected to strike the right balance between development speed and reliability by using engineering solutions to resolve operational issues.

SREs and Automation

According to a reliable survey conducted recently, the most important skill an SRE must have is automation. 92% of the SREs found automation to be the top technical skill required and 18% have indicated that their teams have automated all possible aspects of the operations process. A typical aspect of an SRE is a strong desire not to see the same issue again. This is because the issue has been automized the second time around. SRE participation in problem-solving is more dynamic as they are expected to engineer away the issues rather than just restoring the system back to normalcy. If you find that mobiles and pagers are not ringing continuously on the floor, the SREs have done their job. It means that the system is more stable and reliable, and it is time to move on to another system in the company that needs SREs.

However, you need to remember that SRE is not totally about automation. The engineers require lots of both technical and non-technical skills. The survey indicates that the SRE needs the ability to solve problems, be part of a team, work under pressure, and have strong verbal and written skills. The technical skills required include logging, monitoring, automation, infrastructure configuration, observability, scripting languages and application, and network protocols.

SREs have accepted both continuous deployment and cloud. About 65% of SREs are in the cloud and are deploying codes at least once daily. 47% deploy codes multiple times daily while 27% use it once a week. Another point to remember for the SREs is that it is a position for an experienced engineer and not for an entry level pro. 80% of SREs have been working for more than 6 years, have a college degree, and come with IT Operations experience. Before becoming an SRE, most engineers came from system admin, development, or DevOps background.

Reporting

SREs report mainly to the engineering and operations department. However, it can be noted that SREs report more to software engineering than IT operations. This is slightly surprising as most SREs hail from an IT operations background. 25% of SREs admitted to having more than 100 such engineers under their wings. Google, for example, has 2500 SREs throughout their company. Google is looking at them to create a reliable platform and infrastructure that allows both their indigenous infrastructure and that of their GCP clientele to be stable.

SREs work in close quarters with product development software engineers. They can either be embedded with independent product development teams or separate teams working in close relations and are looking to improve maintainability and reliability. Any company that is looking to improve their software operations will benefit from building an SRE infrastructure and hiring these engineers.

If the surveys conducted are to be believed, the work culture shift can be a hindrance. Moving the job from conventional OPS to SRE can be a difficult cultural shift, not just for the engineers but also for the departments and teams involved in the change. People are still working through the transition and are still finding that the change is far more effective than before and the presence of SREs definitely provides more effective methodology than the IT OPS. Another important factor is the availability as important service indicators, notifications and alerting solutions, as they play a significant role in the tools SREs possess.

2. Principles of SRE

1. Embracing Risk

People might start expecting Google to build a 100% reliable service. The sort of platform and service that will never fail. But the fact of the matter is that increasing reliability after a certain point is not good for the service. The simple reason is that extreme reliability comes at a cost. The stability pushes the development of new features and how fast they can be delivered to users. This again increases the cost. As a result, the team will be forced to reduce the features the maker can offer. Keeping this in mind, the SRE seeks to balance the risk of feature unavailability with rapid innovation and effective operations so that the user's overall happiness with the features, service, and product performance is increased. Unreliable systems quickly lessen the confidence of the users in the system. Remember, as a system is built the cost does not always increase linearly with reliability.

Service reliability management can be expensive as risk management is always costly. 100% reliability is probably not even a good target. Not only is it impossible to achieve, but it is also more dependability than users wish. Always match the service profile with the risk the business is ready to take. An error budget emphasizes the joint ownership between product development and SRE and aligns the incentives. It makes things easier in terms of release dates rate. It also diffuses tense discussions with stakeholders and allows teams to reach the same conclusion.

2. Service Level Objectives (SLOs)

It is not possible to manage a service accurately, let alone well, without knowing which behavior matters for the service and how to evaluate these behaviors. Due to this, we are required to define and provide a certain level of service to the users whether they are using internal API or public products. We need to use experience, understanding of user requirements, and hunch when we are defining the Service Level Objectives (SLOs). The measurements thus derived describe the basic properties of matrices which are significant. Now, what values you wish the matrices to have depend on what the expected service levels are and whether you can provide the level of service. Selection of the right matrices ultimately helps in driving in the right action in case something goes wrong. It also provides necessary confidence to the SRE team that the service is indeed good and healthy.

3. Eliminating Toil

This is one of the most important tasks to be performed by the SRE team. There is always this tendency to toil and to perform repetitive and mundane operational work providing no additional value and scaling linearly with service growth. In case all members of a team are committed to eliminating some toil every week with some quality engineering we are on the way to cleaning up the services and shift the collective efforts towards engineering for scale, development of next generation of services, and building tool chains that are cross SRE. The idea is to invent more and toil less.

4. Monitoring Distributed Systems

If you consider Google or any other empire, monitoring is an absolutely essential part of doing things right during production. In case you can't monitor a service you are at a loss and don't know what is happening. And if you are not aware of what is happening, you cannot be reliable. The SRE teams of Google are aware of the best principles and practices for building useful alerting and monitoring systems. A good alerting and monitoring system is always simple and easy to reason with.

5. Automation

Evolution of automation is a force

multiplier for the SRE. However, multiplying forces does not automatically mean that the force is being applied at the right place. Doing automation mindlessly creates many problems and sometimes these problems are more than the process solves. Although it is a fact that software-based automation is better than a manual one, in most cases, it is better not to have either of the two options. A higher level system design is an autonomous system and it requires neither. In other words, the value of automation is not only in what it does but also in its wise application.

6. Release Engineering

Release engineering is not treated seriously by most companies and is an afterthought in most cases. But release engineering is critical to the overall stability of the system. Remember, most outages occur due to pushing some sort of changes or the others. It is the best way to make sure that all releases are consistent. Release engineering is a comparatively newer and faster-growing side of software engineering. It is useful in building and delivering software. Release engineers require deep knowledge of many domains, such as configuration management, development, system admin, testing, and support. Having reliable services needs you to have reliable release processes. Changes to any feature of the release procedure should be deliberate rather than unintended. SREs take care of the process from the stage of source code to its deployment. At Google, release engineering is a particular job function.

Release engineers work with the software engineers during product development and along with SREs, they decide the steps needed for the software release. Release engineers are involved in how software is stowed in source code repository to shape rules for assembling, testing, packaging and conducting of deployment.

7. Simplicity

One of the key principles of effective software engineering is simplicity. Once this quality is lost it is very difficult to recover and recapture. The simplicity of the software is a pre-requisite to the reliability of the service. We are not being lazy when every task allotted is simplified by us. Rather we will clarify what we are trying to achieve and what is the simplest way to do it. Every time there is a "NO" from the SRE to a feature they are not restricting innovation instead, they are keeping out the cluttered distractions so that the focus remains on innovation and real engineering can move forward.

3. SRE Practices

1. Being On-Call

Constantly being on call is a duty that is critical to several engineering and operations teams in order to undertake their responsibilities. It keeps the team services available and reliable. But there are many problems with organizations having on-call rotations and responsibilities which may lead to dire consequences to the service and for the team in case it's not handled in time. Google's approach to the on-call has enabled the SREs to use engineering work as the means for scaling production responsibilities and maintaining high reliability and availability. This is despite the ever-increasing complexity of the systems and their number.

2. Emergency Response

Things break in the real world. That's life. Regardless of the size of the company or the stakes involved, there is one aspect critical to the long-term health of a company. It also sets an organization apart from others. It is the emergency response and how the people involved react to an emergency. There are a few people who naturally respond well to an emergency. A proper response takes training and preparation. Establishment of training and testing processes needs the support of board and management in addition to staff attention. All these things are necessary for creating an environment in which teams can work towards ensuring processes, systems, and people respond correctly and promptly during an emergency.

3. Learning from Failure: The Postmortem Culture

SREs work with complex, large-scale and well-distributed systems. There is a constant enhancement with new features and addition of new systems. Outages and incidents are pretty much inevitable given the velocity of change and the magnitude of operations. Whenever there is an incident, SREs fix the undermining issue and the services are returned to their normal operational conditions. However, unless there is a process of learning from the outages in place, they will recur many times. If they are left unchecked, they occur in a cascading effect or increase in complexity eventually overwhelming the operator and the system itself affecting end users. For these reasons, a postmortem is an essential tool for SREs. It is a well-known concept in the tech industry. It is a written record of incidents, actions taken and the impact, root causes, and follow-up actions taken to prevent the outage from happening again.

4. Handling Overload

Avoiding overload in a process is a global load balancing policy. However, no matter how well balanced your load balancing policy is, some part of the system at some stage gets overloaded. Handling the overload conditions comfortably is a basic thing in running a reliable service. One way for handling overload is by serving degraded responses. These responses are not as accurate as the normal responses or they have less data than normal but they are easier to compute. But under extreme overload, the service cannot compute, even the degraded responses. At the point, there is no other way than having errors. However, it is critical to ensure that independent tasks are secured against the overload. Take the degraded conditions seriously. If they are ignored, many systems exhibit bad behavior.

5. Data Processing Pipelines

The periodic pipelines in a service are valuable. But if the data processing problem grows organically or is continuous, never use the periodic pipeline. Rather use the technology having characteristics similar to the Workflow. It is a fact that continuous data processing with a strong guarantee like that provided by the Workflow performs well. It also scales well on distributed cluster infrastructure and regularly produces reliable results. It is stable and a reliable system for the SRE team to maintain and manage.

6. Tracking Outages

Improving the reliability of a system is possible only if you start from a baseline and can make a progress. There are devices available to track outages. Learning from past issues systematically is necessary for effective service management. Postmortems provide details on the reports of independent outages. However, they are only a part of the answer. This is because they are written for a larger impact and the smaller issues having frequent but smaller impact and do not fall under their scope. Postmortems provide great insights for improving services but they may miss opportunities to provide similar insight in smaller individual cases. Or some other poor cost-benefit ratios. There is other information such as how many alerts did a team get during their shift, which might point to some useful information. Other similar information such as how many alerts were actionable and how many were non-actionable also provide insight into some issues. "Which services that a team is managing is producing the maximum toil?", also gives some useful information.

7. Reliable Product Launches

Internet companies such as Google can launch new products and features in great speed with rapid iterations than compared to the conventional companies. The role of SRE in the process is to make the rapid change of pace possible without compromising the site stability. Google has created a dedicated team of "Launch Coordination Engineers" for the purpose. They consult with the various engineering teams regarding the technical aspects of the software launch. They create a launch checklist with common questions about the launching and try to resolve issues. The checklist has proved to be a reliable tool for ensuring dependable launches.

4. SRE Implementation

1. Context vs. Control in SRE

One of the most important thing to focus on in SRE is providing context instead of utilizing processes that are working around control. But that is the way most SRE operates. So, what is context versus control in SRE? By context it is meant providing additional and relevant information which allows an engineer to understand the rationalism behind any request. At a higher level the context related to availability is availability of micro services and how they relate to a desired goal including the availability of dependencies. With context fixed to a certain domain, the engineering team will have the responsibility to take steps to improve availability.

On the other hand, in the control-based model an engineering team will be aware of the microservices availability target, but if they fail to achieve the target there might be some punitive action. These actions may involve their ability to push the code to production. It is always better to share context on microservices availability rather than working with teams when availability has to be improved. The challenge is to provide sufficient context to teams. Whenever a non-ideal decision is made at the operations, the first query is, did the person have enough context to make a better decision?

In a big company it is difficult to provide sufficient context so that based on the context alone the personnel can achieve the targets of their service. In these large organizations you may have to fall back on lots of processes to reach availability goals. However, there are some cases for the control-based models. Such as in case where lives are at stake such as in case if someone is writing unsafe software for the autopilot system of an airplane. It is upto the SRE team to decide how much risk they can take in selecting one factor out of control versus context-based models.

2. Building SRE Team

The teams are built to achieve certain objectives, and they could be winning games, launching a product, or implementing a vision. Irrespective of the field we choose, the result must be the same. There are some ways you can take to build a high performing SRE team, although building a team of high performers is a difficult task. The objective of building such a team is to reach a certain degree of operational excellence. You need to build a team that takes care of performance, availability, change management, monitoring, and emergency response and plan the services.

SRE was Google's answer to system admin Operations. The thought process they used for this was, as we are doing software development well, why we can't adapt the same practices to run the Operations section as well? And it turned out to be a very successful thought. Google saw both Dev and Ops teams on the same side. They understood the targets and objectives very well and as a result were able to make good decisions as the features were released. The main difference was how the company was structured. If the Devs and Ops were paid for competing goals, then they will not work together well as a team. Operations is an area of stability and the people are compensated for things such as availability and uptime. Devs on the other hand are rewarded for feature releases, which may contradict with the operations team by lowering availability.

Google was one of the first companies to realize this. Rather than placing two teams on the opposite side of the process, better results can be obtained by having them share a common goal of releasing features with reliability. DevOps and SREs are all different people assembled together for attaining a common objective. There is no fixed definition for going about things. You are required to come up with your own principles as you go along, depending on the setup.

3. Using Incident Metrics to Improve SRE at Scale

It doesn't matter whether you are looking to add a dozen users next or a million users, you are going to end up in a discussion about which areas to invest in and where to stay reliable as the services scale up. Let's look at a case study by using incident metrics to stay focused on investments. Microsoft Azure worked on the lessons that were learned while working on the service reliability ranging from startups to enterprise level to cloud scale.

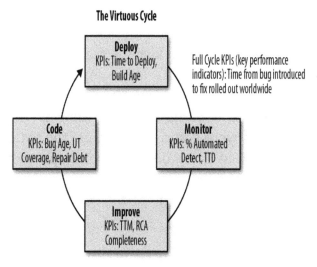

The Virtuous Cycle

a. The Virtuous Cycle

The SRE team began by looking at the data similar to any other issue resolving effort. However, when it was attempted, it turned out that there were thousands of data sources, incident management metrics, service telemetry, and deployment metrics, and so on. It made things tricky as it had to be decided which data to look at and in what order. After consulting the experts and after looking at the best available practices, the SRE team landed on a system called The Virtuous Cycle. It created a framework which allowed the SRE team to see how useful monitoring was by finding out how fast the team detected the outages. It also depended on measuring the root-cause analysis process, repairs, and how quickly the issues were getting fixed. Then the team looked at the code quality and speed of deployment to see how quickly they would run through the full cycle.

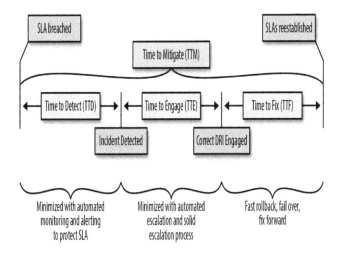

The SRE team was fully aware of how much downtime matters, so they began looking at the key metrics. They told the team how effective they were to responding to incidents and fixing them. It also meant that first, they had to define metrics that were representative of the information needed. Then agree upon definitions and timings. You could have different definitions or metrics but the group must agree on common measures and taxonomy. Agreement on taxonomy was particularly important as there might have been disconnects otherwise.

b. Metrics Review

After all these metrics were defined, the key SREs were called to look at the significant metrics that were identified as crucial to drive the virtuous cycle. Then the team tracked how they were progressing and created action plans in areas they were hitting targets. After agreeing on the metrics, the team started collecting data on how they were doing and found areas and common areas for improvement and measured the impact made by the improvements later.

The next figure shows an example of the dashboard to measure deployment and incident metrics. It allowed the team to track the trend for incident response cycle and engineer improvements in the same way as features are engineered in the product. All the incident response metrics discussed earlier show up in the figure. They measure against the targets we set and agreed on with the service owners. In case the data was found to be too much with high variability, or had too many outliers, the team applied percentile to it to normalize it enough. The outliers made it easier to understand and drive the percentile close to 100%.

	Period 1	Period 2	Period 3	Period 4	Period 5	Period 6	Trend	Goal
Σ Incidents	XX	XX	XX	XX	XX	XX.XXX%		
Σ Major Incidents	X	X	X	X	X	X		
SLO	XX.XXX%	XX.XXX%	XX.XXX%	XX.XXX%	XX.XXX%	XX.XXX%		XX.XX%
TTD @ XX%ile	XX	XX	XX	XX	XX	XX		<X min
TTE @ XX%ile	XX	XX	XX	XX	XX	XX		<XX min
TTF @ XX%ile	XX	XXX	XX	XXX	XX	XX		<XX min
TTM @ XX%ile	XX	XXX	XX	XXX	XX	XX		<XX min
% Outages autodetected	XX%	XX%	XX%	XX%	XX%	XX%		XX%
# DRIs engaged per Bridge	XX	X	XX	X	XX	XX		X
DRI Hops	X	X	X	X	X	X		X

Top Incidents	Cause	TTD (mins)	TTM (mins)	Repair Items	Impact (reported)	Impact (Actual)
Incident in North Europe due to Code Bug	Code Bug	XX	XX	1	2	XXX Accounts Impacted
Network Incident due to Configuration	Config	X	XX	4	0	X,XXX Accounts Impacted

Deployment	95% of clusters		100% of clusters	
	Build Age	Build Age Trend	Build Age	Build Age Trend
Service A	XX		XXX	
Service B	XX		XX	

In the SRE metrics dashboard, there are many surrogate metrics such as DRI

41

hops, which indicate how many on-call engineers are necessary to solve an incident. Auto detection gives you the figures for the incidents that are detected via monitoring. These are more actionable than the top level metrics but don't indicate success by themselves.

c. Repair Debt

A lot of insight that was derived out of the metrics review was available from post-incident review procedure. Every time a team member identifies a bug for repair it is logged. Repair items are fixed later, which prevents an outage from happening or reduces its duration. They are divided as short-term items or long-term items. The short-term items are rolled out faster within a week and they might be a script, a process, or even a hotfix. The long-term objects are more lasting fixes such as thorough code fixes, and create broader process change. The repair items are tracked in the same management system used for tracking work management. However, what is significant is that they are logged, reportable, and distinguishable in the product backlog. Repair item tracking allows us to incorporate an operational debt in the engineering procedure and treat it like feature work.

d. Real-Time Dashboards

Probably the most significant part of a metrics review is to bring the insights and metrics into real-time dashboards. If you look at the data weekly or monthly it doesn't help to drive the changes quick enough. All the services and components need to be seen and evaluated in real time where they are working, where they are performing well, and where they could improve. Dashboards have to be created which can be pivoted by a service or a manager even down to an engineer that owns the item.

Conclusion

In a nutshell, you need to measure everything, be curious, and do not be afraid to get your hands dirty and dip into the data to find the right things to do. In many cases getting these insights needed a lot of data to be hand curated but the team understood which metrics mattered and they could automate and instrument them to help bring visibility to the metrics and help services to get better.

4. SREs Working with Third Parties

No app can be completed without third parties. Most IT professionals find them a pain to deal with but lovely for their business, and they are fantastic for marketing. None of the companies know exactly how many 3rd party applications they have and what their value addition is. They are also not aware of the harm they could do to the performance, functionality, or security of the app. Developers are constantly challenged to add code and yet ensure that they don't break anything or start security holes and keep the app functional at all times.

5. From SysAdmin to SRE

The classical role of a system admin is defined generically as IT operations staff which is responsible for building, designing, and maintaining a company's computer infrastructure. The IT world is growing and changing constantly, and the role of SysAdmin is getting limited to hosting platforms and he can do it easily by applying policy around the server instance. Businesses are constantly changing these days and more and more of them are going towards Lean methodologies to achieve the efficiency they desire. The next stages of tech development mean the server administration gets tougher for manual operators and the infrastructure is delivered by a coded workflow. In such a case, you need to hire people who write the code. This is where SREs come in. These engineers know about data structures and programming languages along with algorithms. They can review the performance properly along with instrumenting and measuring it while running. Along with the software skills they have the know-how of the operational management, which ensures that the software has given capabilities throughout its operational life. These include resistance to failure, server, and site, scalability that can accommodate changing workloads and security patch management.

Several sysadmins have come into practice, having evolved from different sources such as help desk, support, or even just running computer systems at home. However, this evolutionary path will not work for the transition from sysadmin to SRE. The main reason for this is that the SRE require software skills and to understand the application itself, and you need to have learned these skills in a structured way. Learning programming at any level is a good starting point and the more you look at programming, the more you start to understand the developer's viewpoints. Several businesses in this world are on a journey of evolution and only a handful of them need SREs now. But all infrastructures will benefit from the fact that their sysadmin has software skills. All sysadmins need to follow this path.

6. DevOps vs. Site Reliability Engineering

As technology evolves, so too do the new roles in organizations and the level of expertise. There are two terms which have become buzzwords thanks mainly to Google branding, and they are Site Reliability Engineers and DevOps. The question is, do the responsibilities considered under the titles represent anything new or modern? Is there any real value to these roles or are they just buzzwords to further resumes?

There is enough contradiction about the titles as it is, and it has opened a debate on what their functions are and what is the difference among them. There are some people who take a hard look at the roles and come up with the summary that they are basically the same thing. Well, there is a lot in common, especially when you consider the undermining objectives such as automation, scaling, bridging the gap between development, and operations. However, there is a clear difference between them.

There are dynamic companies who wish to scale at an aggressive speed who will look to lay a foundation for an IT department which is supple and agile. To do this they will need engineering departments that can create foundations for supporting the targets. The directors of these teams will need to leverage the automation tools to enable widespread conducting of infrastructure and management to several teams. There are two main branches here to perform this. One is SRE which is clearly defined to create a fully automated IT infrastructure. The DevOps, on the other hand, is more an orchestration of a Lean or Agile development team. They serve infrastructure as the code to the programmers when required.

The IT infrastructure is pretty often built piece by piece as the organization grows. The systems are built to serve company objectives from day one. Changes will be made later as they are required. Sysadmin plays a critical role in ensuring that the daily maintenance and system updates are created to protect the investments and keep a productive environment. The admins spend their day ensuring that everything is working correctly in the company. They also ensure that everything is updated and the address breaks are there when required.

There are more sophisticated IT teams which can engineer automation scripts in the infrastructure from the beginning, removing future reliance on admin. The system architect or engineer can orchestrate patches, policy, and management over the whole network via a single CMS (Centralized Management System). These systems monitor the environment proactively and detect potential anomalies within the infrastructure before they become anomalies.

SREs are more focused on the system architect's role in core infrastructure. This is more linked to the production environment. DevOps are more related to automation and simplification of development teams and their non-production environments. The major difference between an SRE and DevOps is that the focus is on coding and the kind of environment you are placed in. DevOps will always be on the creation and testing side as they are dynamic departments and use the Lean or Agile methodology to run their operations. Also, there must be automation to help manage the processes.

Developers use automation tools such as Chef or Puppet to help with the challenges. DevOps share some common factors with SRE as well. The DevOps engineer is at the top of the pyramid architecting both a system and a culture to automate the delivery of infrastructure or other work in the development process. The main theme here is that both these new roles that are SRE and DevOps are being used to help the service run more efficiently. As we move forward, we typically expect the practices to evolve and new roles will be created. What is significant is that what drives the change is operationally efficient and is fully contingent. These forms help in supporting innovation with better speed and also aid the departments to run and scale more fluidly as a whole.

7. Production Engineering at Facebook

The production engineering lifecycle at Facebook is how they build, run, and disband their great reliability focused teams along with performance, scalability, and efficiency. It was started in 2009 with a handful of engineers in a single office. Now there are several hundreds of engineers that support dozens of teams in four countries and 6 offices. When Facebook production engineers are hired they have to be good coders in at least one shell language. They need to know TCP/IP Networking, Linux Systems, Distributed systems design, and debugging, reliability engineering background and be available on call.

5. SRE Processes and Best Practices

In simple terms, SREs run services by using a set of networked systems, operated for users that might be internal and external. They are also responsible for the wellbeing of these services. Operating a service successfully means a wide range of activities, such as planning capability, monitoring, responding to incidents, making sure that the root causes for the outages are systematically addressed, etc.

SREs represent a break away from the current industry best practices for managing difficult and large services. The SRE was originally influenced by software engineering, but now SRE methodologies have become a different set of principles, practices, and a set of incentives in the field of DevOps area of expertise.

Some key SRE nest practices are:

• Support the services before they

are live via activities like developing software frameworks and platforms, system design consulting, launch reviews, and capacity planning.

- Engaging in improving the complete life cycle of services. This means from inception and design stage to deployment, operations, and refinement.

- Maintenance of services when they are live by monitoring and measuring the availability, latency, and overall health of the system.

- Practicing incident response that is sustainable and quality postmortems.

- Scaling of systems via mechanisms such as automation, and evolution of systems by pushing the necessary changes to improve speed and reliability.

The networking technology addresses several challenges that are associated with SREs and their best practices. In order to assure optimum network performance and network operations, the SRE team needs a detailed and correct application and networking insight to ensure system performance and availability.

1. Handling Overload

Avoiding the overload condition is the target for load balancing policies. However, no matter how good your load balancing policy is, eventually some parts of the system become overloaded. Handling overload conditions gracefully is a fundamental requirement in running any reliable serving system. It is also important that individual tasks are also protected against overload conditions. For example, a backend task serving a certain traffic rate should continue to keep doing so at the same rate without any impact on the latency. This needs to continue despite how much surplus traffic is added at the task.

The backend chore should not fall over and crash while placed under the load. The statements must hold true for a definite rate of traffic which is 2X or even 10X of what the task is allotted to process. It is an accepted fact that at a certain point the system will break down and rising the point at which the breakdown occurs is very difficult to achieve.

The key to handling overload conditions is to take degradation conditions seriously. If the situations are ignored, various systems display terrible behavior. As work piles up the tasks find it hard to run and they ultimately run out of retention and crash or even might end up burning the CPU. Latency suffers pretty badly as the traffic is dropping and the tasks start competing for resources. If the condition is left unchecked a failure in a subgroup of a system can trigger multiple failures in other system components causing the entire system to fail at some point in time. The impact from this can be so damaging that it is dangerous for any scheme operating at scale to have protection against it.

It is a common misconception that the overloaded backend must turn down and halt accepting all the traffic. This conception goes against the target of robust load balancing. It is better for the backend to keep accepting as much circulation as possible but only accept the load as the memory frees up. A quality backend, if supported by strong load balancing strategies, will accept only those requests it can process gracefully and reject the others.

There are a range of tools available for implementing quality load balancing and overload protection. But they are not magic, as load balancing needs a thorough understanding of systems and the semantics of the requests. There are many techniques used by Google that have evolved and will continue to do so as the nature of systems continue to modify.

2. SRE Engagement Model Evolution

We have discussed so far what happens when the SRE is already in place and in custody of a service. But very few facilities begin their lifespan enjoying SRE support. Therefore, there is a need to have a process for assessing a service, ensuring that it needs the support of an SRE, a negotiation about how to improve the negative conditions that block SRE support and really have the SREs. This process is called on boarding. In case you are in a situation where you are bounded by many services which are in a different state of completion and excellence, your SRE team is probably running through an ordered queue for onboardings for quite some time. It would have finished taking on the high-value targets by now.

This is a common and totally reasonable method of dealing with such a fait accompli situation. However, there are at least two different ways of bringing in the wisdom gathered from production and SRE care to the services new and old. In the first scenario like software engineering, the earlier an SRE team is consulted the better. It is similar to finding a bug early. The earlier it is found, the cheaper it is to repair it. The earlier an SRE team is consulted the more beneficial it will be. When SREs are engaged early in the stages of design the on boarding time is lowered and the services become more reliable. This is normally because there is no reason to unwind suboptimal design or its implementation.

The second way is perhaps the best way and it involves short-circuiting the process due to which specially fashioned systems having a lot of individual differences end up at the SRE door. Provide the PD team with a platform that is validated by the SRE infrastructure upon which the production team can build their system. The platform will benefit both reliability and scalability. This also avoids some cognitive load issues completely and by addressing the general infrastructure practices it allows the product development team to focus on innovations at application layer stage where it belongs.

It is certain that service reliability can be improved by SRE engagement. It is a process in which there are systematic reviews and improvement of the production process. The SREs initial such approach in Google was Simple Production Readiness Review that went a long way in standardizing the SRE engagement model, but it was applicable only to services that had reached the launching phase. Over a period of time, SREs extended and improved this model.

The earlier engagement model showed SRE involving in the development life cycle earlier as it improved the design for reliability. The demand for SRE expertise has grown since then and a more scalable model is envisaged. Some frameworks were developed for production services to meet this demand. Codes based on the best practices of production were standardized and encapsulated in the framework. So this meant that use of frameworks was recommended, simple, consistent way of building production enables services. Adoption of the framework has become a prominent influence on developing Google's production ready services. They were also responsible for expanding SRE contribution lowering the overheads such as service management and thereby improving baseline service quality of the company.

3. Accelerating the SREs to On-Call and More than That

The trick is to speed up the newbies and at the same time keep the senior SREs up to speed in the process. So, you have hired your set of SREs but now what? Now you need to train them on the work. You need to invest upfront in their education and technical orientation that will hopefully make them better engineers. This kind of training makes them proficient by accelerating their training process. It also makes their skills more balanced, sharp and robust.

The most successful SRE teams are built through mutual trust. In order to maintain any service consistently and universally you are required to trust fellow colleagues to know the system. Not only are they required to know the system, they must be able to diagnose system behavior and they should be available for help easily. They must also react under pressure for saving your day. so SRE education doesn't end at, "What does a newcomer needs to learn to be on-call?" Given the requirements of trust you are also needed to ask questions such as:

- How many current co-workers are assessing the readiness of a newcomer for the on-call role?

- How can we incorporate the enthusiasm and curiosity in the newbies to ensure that the existing SREs benefit from them?

- What are the activities to get the team involved to benefit everyone in terms of their education? Everyone must enjoy the process.

All students have a range of learning preferences. Learning that you will have to hire people who have a mix of these preferences. You will choose someone with one kind of style ignoring other set of expenses. There is no fixed style of education to train new SREs and there is certainly no magic formula that works for the entire SRE team. Below there are some recommended training practices that are well known at the SRE of Google? These represent a huge range of options available to make your team an expert in the SRE concepts, both now and on an ongoing basis.

Here are some recommended patterns,

- Design sequential and concrete learning material/experiences for students. Deluge students off their menial work.

- Encourage statistical thinking, reverse engineering, fundamental, and working principles. Avoid training them strictly through operational procedures, playbooks, and checklists.

- Encourage students to read the failure analysis by suggesting postmortems. Avoid efforts to bury the outages to conceal the blame.

- Create realistic breakages allowing students to fix them with real monitoring and tooling. This avoids students from having the first chance to fix when he is already on-call.

- Encourage role playing with theoretical disasters as a group to improve a team's issue solving ability. Avoid experts being created who are compartmentalized.

- Allow students to shadow on-call

rotations early, thereby allowing them to compare notes with the on-caller. Avoids students from getting to the on-call situation before their knowledge is holistic.

- Pair the student with expert SREs to be able to revise on-call training plans. This stops the thinking that the incident is to be touched by experts only.

- Allow the students partial ownership by giving them nontrivial project work. This nullifies the tendency for the expert to get significant work and the newbie's left cleaning up the scraps.

4. Dealing with Interrupts

The operational load is the work when applied to complex systems must be done in order to maintain a system in a functional state. Viz. in case you own a car, someone will always service it, place gas in it, or do other maintenance work related to it to keep it performing its functionalities. All complex systems are as full of errors as its creators.

There are many forms to operational overloads when they are applied to maintaining complex systems. Some of them are more obvious than others. The terminology used may change but the operational load falls under three categories: tickets, pages, and ongoing operational activities.

Pages: They are related to production alerts and their fallouts. Pages are triggered in response to production emergencies. They are many times recurring and monotonous, needing little thought. They may also be involving and with in-depth tactical thought. These pages have an SLO (expected response time) that is measured in minutes.

Tickets: Tickets are customer requests that ask you to take action. Like pages, tickets may be boring and simple or may need real thinking. One simple ticket may request a code review for a configuration that the team owns or a more complex ticket may entail special requests for help with a decision or capacity plans. Tickets can also have SLO, but in this case, the response time is measured in hours, days, and weeks.

Ongoing Operational Responsibilities: They are also referred to as "Kicking the can down the road" or "Toil". They involve activities such as team owned code or flag rollouts, or responses to sudden situations or time-sensitive queries from clients. Although they do not have a definite SLO these tasks may interrupt you.

There are operational overloads that can be anticipated easily or planned for but most of them are unplanned. It can interrupt someone at any non-specific time requiring the person to make a decision whether it can wait or not.

5. Recovering an SRE from Operational Overload

It is a common policy for the Google SRE team to evenly divide their time between their developments and sensitive ops work. Their balance remains upset for several months due to a surge in daily tickets volume. A massive amount of ops work is particularly dangerous as the SRE team may burn out or become handicapped to make progress on the project at hand. Whenever a team must allocate an uneven amount of time to resolve tickets at the cost of spending time on improving service, its reliability, and scalability suffer.

One way of relieving this burden is by temporarily transferring an additional SRE in the overloaded team. Once this person is embedded in the team, the SRE focuses on improving practices opposed to just helping the team empty the ticket queue. This SRE observes the daily routine of the team and recommends certain points to improve team practices. This adds a fresh perspective to the team performance and their routines that cannot be provided by the team itself.

However, while using this approach, it is necessary to transfer more than a single engineer. Well, two SREs does not necessarily mean better results. It may cause issues in case the team doesn't react suitably to them.

6. Communicating and Collaboration within SRE

The SRE organizational position in Google is stimulating and has a clear effect on how you communicate and collaborate. There is a huge diversity involved in SRE work and how it is done. There are service teams, infrastructure teams, and horizontal product teams. There are relationships involved with product growth teams sometimes much larger than SRE teams and sometimes the same size. Then there are situations in which the SRE team is the product development team. SRE teams are made from people who are equipped with architectural skills or system engineering skills, project management skills, software engineering skills, leadership qualities, and a background in all fields of engineering. They do not have just a single model and they have more than one configuration that work. This flexibility is suitable to their ultimate pragmatic nature.

It is also a fact that the SRE is not your command and control company. Normally they have an alliance with at least two masters, one for service and the other for infrastructure. They work in general SRE context. The relationship with service is very strong as they are held responsible for the show of those systems. However, despite that relationship, the actual reporting lines are via SRE as a whole. Nowadays, the SRE spends more time supporting their independent services across the production work. But they come from shared values culture and, as a result, they have a strong homogeneous approach to the issues. It is so by design.

The facts mentioned above have steered SRE organizations in certain directions whilst taking into consideration two crucial dimensions called communication and collaboration. For communication, the apt computing metaphor will be data flow. Similar to the fact that data must flow around the production, it has to flow around SRE as well. Data could be about the condition of the services, projects, production, and the condition of the persons. For the highest efficiency of a team, service data must move in a reliable way from one point to another. One way of thinking about this flow is by thinking about the interface an SRE team must show to other teams like the APL. Like the APL a good design is critical for the effective operation, and in case the API is incorrect it will be very difficult to correct later on.

The API is also pertinent for collaboration as contract metaphor both for the SRE teams and between product development and SRE teams. They all need to progress in an environment with constant change. This collaboration looks pretty much like collaboration between any other fast-moving organization. The only difference being the mix of system engineering expertise, software engineering skills, and the wisdom gathered out of production that the SRE brings to the collaboration. A best design and best implementation happens when there is a joint concern between production and the invention being met with mutual respect. This happens to be the promise an SRE makes to an organization. They are equipped with dependability, with the similar skills as that of product development teams. This improves things a great deal. Experience indicates that just having a person in charge of consistency without the full skill set will not be enough for the job.

Considering the globally spread nature of SRE teams, effective communication will always be high priority within the SRE. The collaboration within the SRE teams has its challenges but also great rewards, including a common approach to platform for solving issues and allowing the team to focus on more difficult issues.

7. Testing for Reliability

One of the key responsibilities of SREs is to quantify the confidence in the system they are maintaining. This is achieved by SREs adapting the classical software testing techniques at scale to the systems. The confidence can be measured in terms of past reliability and forthcoming reliability. Past is captured by analyzing the data provided via monitoring the system behavior. While the future is quantified by making educated predictions from the data indicated in the past system behavior. To make sure that these predictions are correct to be of use, one of the subsequent conditions must be good:

- The website has remained totally unchanged over a period of time without any software publications or changes in servers. This means that the future behavior of the system will be the same as the past.

- You can confidently tell all changes to the website with the analysis which will follow indicate all uncertainties incurred due to the changes.

Testing is a method used to establish specific areas of similarity when there are changes. Every test that passes before and after the changes reduces the uncertainty factor for which the analysis follows. Thorough testing allows us to predict the reliability of a system with sufficient details to be pragmatically useful. The amount of testing required hinges on the reliability requirements of the system.

As the percentile of codebase covered by tests increases, you are reducing the uncertainty and increase the reliability in the system. Sufficient testing means that you are permitted to make more changes before the reliability falls below a certain acceptable level. In case you make too many changes too fast. the reliability also approaches the acceptability mark quickly. You should stop making any changes at this point while the new data accumulates. This accumulated data supplements the test coverage and validates the reliability asserted for the revised paths of execution. By assuming that the served clients are arbitrarily distributed, the sampling statistics are more reliable. They are extrapolated from the monitored metrics and the aggregate behavior indicates the use of new paths. The statistics identify certain areas that need heavier testing.

8. Software Engineering within SRE

In case you ask someone to title any Google software engineering work, they are likely to name one of the consumer-facing products such as Google Maps or Gmail. Some people may mention the underlying infrastructures such as Colossus or Bigtable. However, the truth is that there is an enormous amount of software engineering that goes on behind the scenes that the consumers never get to see and many of those yields are prepared within SRE.

Google has a production environment which by some way is one of the utmost complex ones that humanity has ever developed. SREs have readymade experience with the nitty-gritty of production. That makes them exceptionally well suited to make the suitable tools required to solve internal issues and use the cases that are related to keeping the production running. The bulk of the tools are connected to the overall objective of maintaining the uptime and keeping the latency low and assume many forms. Examples of this are monitoring, binary rollout mechanisms, or a development setting built on a dynamic server composition.

All-in-all these tools developed by SRE are developed software engineering projects and are different from unique solutions and quick hacks. The SREs that have developed these products have adopted a mindset that is a product based that considers both the internal customers and the roadmap for future plans.

In several ways, the huge measure of the Google production has demanded internal software development. This is mainly because very few third-party tools must be developed at the necessary scale for Google's needs. Google's history of successful projects in software engineering has led many to agree to the doles of developing straight within the SRE. SREs are in a good position to develop this internal software for several reasons.

The software engineering projects in Google SRE have grown with the organization and, in several cases, the lessons that were learned from the successful execution of earlier development projects have paved the way for their subsequent endeavors. The unique and hands-on experience that SREs have brought to the development tools leads to innovative approaches to the conventional issues. The SRE driven projects are clearly beneficial to the organization in creating a successful model for supporting the services at scale. As SREs often develop software to streamline the inefficient processes or automate common tasks. The projects mean that the SRE teams do not have to scale linearly with the size of the services they are supporting. In the end, the benefits of having the SRE devoting some of their time to software development are always reaped by the organization.

9. Load Balancing at the Front End/in the Datacenter

Google serves several million requirements every second at the front end. Obviously, they use more than just a single computer for handling all these requests. However, even if there was a single super computer that was someway able to handle all the requirements at the same time, Google will still not employ a policy that relies on a single point failure. When you are dealing with systems that are so big, placing all your eggs in a single basket is a sure recipe for disaster. Now let us consider load balancing within the datacenter. Application level policies are used for routing the requests onto individual servers which can process them.

10. Managing a Critical State

It is a reality that processes crash or need to be resumed. Hard drives also fail. Natural disasters are responsible for taking out many datacenters in a region. SREs are required to anticipate these kinds of disasters and develop strategies which will run the service despite calamities. The strategies usually means running these systems on several websites. Distributing a system geographically is relatively straightforward but it involves maintaining a consistent view of the state of the system which is indeed difficult and a nuanced undertaking. There are groups of processes which may wish to agree reliably on the following queries:

- Which is the leader of the group process?

- What is the state of processes involved in a group?

- Does the process hold lease?

- Has the message been committed successfully to the distribute queues?

- What is the given key's value in a data store?

Distributed consensus is very effective in building highly available and reliable systems that need a constant view of some state of the system. The distributed consensus means reaching an agreement amongst a collection of processes linked by an unreliable network. For example, many processes in a scattered system are needed to form a constant view of a critical configuration. This is despite whether the distributed lock is seized or the message in the queue is processed or not.

Keep in mind the kind of problems the distributed consensus can be used to solve. Also remember the kinds of problems that can arise when ad hoc methods like heartbeats are utilized instead of the distributed consensus. When you see critical shared state, leader election, or distributed locking always think of distributed consensus. Any lesser approach will be a ticking bomb waiting to explode in the system.

6. Building SRE Success Culture at LinkedIn (A Case Study)

Being an SRE (Site Reliability Engineer) means having to face a lot of tough problems. Complex failure scenarios, outages, and other technical crises are amongst the things they must be ready to deal with every working day at LinkedIn. When they are not dealing with problems they are discussing them. They perform regular postmortems and root cause analysis and they are required to dig into difficult technical difficulties in an unflinching and relentless way.

Strangely enough, discussing culture in an SRE association can be a lot harder. At LinkedIn, it is constantly discussed how the culture is equally as important as their products. And yet it is tough to have a blueprint for other teams and companies to aid them in creating the right SRE culture. One wishes there were easy steps to follow in the technology industry. Things like range and inclusion are common in the tech world. As things are, there are several companies looking to generate a positive culture but are not always sure how to go on board the process.

1. Postmortem on the SRE Culture at LinkedIn

They are certainly not claiming that they have found a formula that fit all the processes for creating the correct engineering culture. But two engineers from the team told their boss that they feel the LinkedIn culture is exclusive and as an employee they felt valued and supported despite their backgrounds.

This caused the writer to reflect on SRE organization culture specifically because he knew that things were not like that always. He has mentioned below some changes they made over the years for installing an all-inclusive culture, a positive attitude, and discussion of activities performed on a daily basis. And to maintain the procedures.

Although this is not a specific guide some of the thoughts and their experiences are sure to benefit those looking to change the organizational culture.

2. Fighting Fire in the Early Years

In the earlier years of the SRE team, they were not even called SREs. Their role was more of a mixture of firefighting, release management, and conventional operations. The focus was completely on getting these things done and there was no culture to speak of. Now, the LinkedIn site was infused with many reliability issues as it was faced with hyper growth. All the tech team could think of was to keep things going. There was no time to think of the culture they were creating, technically or otherwise.

When things finally leveled up a little, they decided that they needed to make grave changes to the team to correct the various issues with the product. They reorganized themselves as an SRE team and tasked themselves with a clear goal in mind and that was to keep the website up and running all the time. In order to align with this assignment, they decided to embrace values of ownership and craftsmanship across engineering. This meant they felt totally responsible for the site like they were the owners of it. They viewed their functions as a craft, which requires execution.

This overhaul to an extent was successful. The site was moved into a more stable position and the role of the operations team to solve the issues was made via software instead of people and process.

3. Dealing with the Culture Debt

Like all the SREs, the LinkedIn team SREs are always thoughtful about things such as efficiency, resilience, automation, and the availability of team member experience. When you are tackling these issues everyday you are working with other teams or other SREs in a larger engineering organization. So we need SREs that are aware of the importance of collaboration with other people.

As the LinkedIn technical situation was terrible during their hyper growth period, they have come to value their technical skills above all in their management and hiring processes. Rather than considering whether candidates will be people that will be great teammates in the long-run, they placed more importance on their technical capabilities and how they could help in the short-term. Although, this got them some very talented individuals it also revealed certain flaws over a period. Having engineers who not exactly great team players were made the collaborative work more difficult. The work is a vital part of site reliability. In many cases it created a negative work atmosphere. After a while the experience became so painful for everyone involved that a need for change was observed. This was similar to how a technical debt builds up in a long lived code base. Over a period they made specific changes to their philosophy, people, and their processes in the SRE. This is how they solved the cultural debt that was built over time.

4. Philosophy

The head of engineering and operations at LinkedIn was David Hanke, who began promoting the SREs to have a mindset of attacking the problem and not the person involved. The SRE team's daily work is to constantly identify and correct issues and bugs. So it is vital to remember that we are all on the same team and are fighting against outages. It fostered a culture of equality and inclusion in the SRE team's mindset. So, whenever there was an outage, it was not considered as my problem, but our problem and we are all together to fix it.

5. People

In 2013 LinkedIn invested plenty of effort into formalizing and evolving their SREs interview process. Part of the process was explicitly looking for the missing collaborative spirit they wished their engineers displayed. This was of course in addition to technical abilities. Slowly this began to build their ranks with people who fit this culture as they were not just equipped technically but became a part of the culture. By the time this level of maturity was reached in the hiring process there were around 100 people in the SRE team. It was a far cry from those handful of people that started out in the earlier years. As the organization grew the ability to collaborate successfully became more tied directly to technical work. Not focusing on the quality of new hires only functioned for a while, as they were a smaller company.

6. Process

Nowadays the LinkedIn SRE team consists of hundreds of SRE engineers located in different geographic locations. To have scaling culture along with a team is challenging, but what really helps them a great deal is that their leadership is aligned towards the environment they wish to create. Everyone knows the significance of having a cooperative and all-inclusive culture and so it is their priority to preserve it. Part of it is by reinforcing the values in the daily stand up meeting.

Each day, the SRE goes along with anybody who wishes to participate in a short conference or go over website reliability issues from the past 24 hours and the immediate preventive fixes that are being implemented for every incident. As these topics are being discussed, they ensure that a solution is approached not only from a technical standpoint but from a cultural point of view. For example, if a defensive behavior is observed, they will tell the team to attack the issue and not the person. Or, in case an outage was because of a breakdown in communication, time is taken to re-emphasize that they are all on an identical team and need to see each other in the same light.

One part of these conferences is that the culture is not made a separate aspect on its own. It is always integrated in the way the problems of the day, such as recurring bugs or site outages, are discussed. As a result, you are doing your job correctly from the technical perspective and are following cultural values as well. The two are moving ahead healthily as they are intertwined.

7. Conclusion

They don't make-believe to be perfect and understand that there is still a lot of work to be done. But hearing fellow SREs say that they are treated well and with equality makes the manager feel that they are moving in the right direction. These examples, such as hiring for cultural fitting or making cultural and procedural values consistent and reinforcing these standards daily, can help create a culture you want to see in an organization.

7. SRE & DevOps: Similarities & Differences

So, how is it going? Though I have passed on useful information regarding SRE Principles, Processes, Implementation and case studies, there is one important topic I wanted to cover. There are many views and definitions on the similarities and differences of DevOps and SRE .Lets collate them and see how it shapes up!

So, while taking the SRE and DevOps names in one go, this is what the subject matter experts are saying about both of them!

1. About DevOps:

- The core reason for DevOps movement to start was the lack of production exposure of coders. They were writing codes without any idea of what the other guy in the production environment goes through.

91

- DevOps is more of an organizational culture which fills the gap between coder and the operation person and aligns them to the overall organizational goal.

- Overall DevOps culture is abstract class which leaves the implementation details to be customized by the author.

2. About SRE:

- SRE is what happens when a software engineer is entrusted with operations!

- SRE was developed by Google for internal consumption and overlaps with the DevOps culture and philosophy. But, the SRE is more explicit and measures and achieves reliability. Overall, SRE advice the way forward *to achieve the reliability and success in various DevOps areas.*

3. Differences

- The major difference in the

problem solving approach is that DevOps team raises the problem and sends it to Dev to solve, where as the SRE team take the ownership of solving it too.

- SRE team is more confident in handling the production environment where as DevOps team doesn't interfere often with the production. Also, improving operational efficiency and performance is one of the goals of a SRE.

- SRE is an approach where the coders are given the ownership to deploy, monitor and maintain the application releases. SRE philosophy believes in taking charge and deploying developers who have operations mindset, whereas DevOps believes in bridge the dev and op gap by aligning the goals of the teams with that of the organization.

4. Is it bird, plane or Superman! Are we doing DevOps or SRE?

- According to many companies that implemented SRE in a slightly different way than Google, you don't have to decide. At Reedit, ops engineers work on reducing toil, improving deployment and scaling processes, but they are referred to as "DevOps."

- One more example can be taken of Logz.io which defined the role as DevOps and not SRE: "They fill the gap between coders and operations through automated monitoring and performance stress- testing".

5. Similarities

Both SRE and DevOps are aiming for:

- Monitor and Measure the success

- Move from Silos to collaboration between Dev & Ops Teams

- Move towards Organizational Culture more accepting of failures

- Automation

6. DevOps Pillars vs. SRE Practices

DevOps	SRE
Measure	availability, uptime, outages, toil, etc. is measured
Reduce Silos	Same tools & techniques are used by developers and ops

Accept Failure	Formula for containing & balancing failures in new releases
Automation	Minimizing manual work for long term value addition
Gradual Change	Do fail and move ahead quickly to reduce cost of failure

Conclusion

As the SRE industry has grown, there are a couple of different dynamics that have come into play. First are the consistent primary responsibilities of the SRE and the concerns over a period of time. Systems might be 1000 times faster or larger but the real need is for them to remain reliable, easy to manage in case of emergencies, and flexible. They also need to be well monitored and have their capacities planned. At the same time, normal activities undertaken by the SREs have evolved as Google services and other company products have matured. For example, once upon a time for Google a goal was to build a single dashboard for twenty machines. Now it is an automatic discovery. Just get to dashboard building and alert a fleet of thousands of machines at a time.

An SRE team must be as compact as possible. It should operate at a great degree of abstraction in the process relying on many backup systems as failsafes along with APIs to collaborate with the systems. The SRE team must have solid knowledge of the systems and how they work. They must also know how they fail and how they must respond to these failures. This comes from working on those failures day to day.

Most practices and principles used by Google for SRE are evident across a range of industries out there. The lessons learned by established industries have inspired several other practices in use today. The significance of outages can be vital to many industries. For example, people could get injured or even die if there is an outage in the case of some industries such as medical, aviation, or nuclear. When the stakes are very high there has to be a conservative approach as the reliability is of paramount importance.

If we consider an industry such as Google, there is a constant tightrope between high reliability expected by users and the sharp focus on innovation and rapid changes. Google is unbelievably serious about reliability and they create approaches for the high rate of change. Of course, in many cases, the reliability of term reliability is also taken into consideration.

** How did you like the book? Could you spare some time and review it.

My Other Books available across the platforms in e-book, paperback and audible versions:

1. **Blockchain Technology : Introduction to Blockchain Technology and its impact on Business Ecosystem**

2. DevOps Handbook: Introduction to DevOps and its Impact on Business Ecosystem

3. Blockchain Technology and DevOps : Introduction and Impact on Business Ecosystem

4. **Love Yourself: 21 day plan for learning "Self-Love" to cultivate self-worth ,self-belief, self-confidence & happiness**

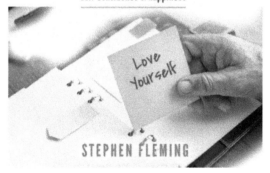

7 EFFECTIVE TECHNIQUES OF

INTERMITTENT FASTING

**Stay Healthy,Lose Weight,
Slow Down Aging Process & Live Longer!**

STEPHEN FLEMING

6. Love Yourself and intermittent Fasting(Mind and Body Bundle Book)

New Releases 2018

You can check all my Books on my **Amazon's Author Page**

** If you prefer audible versions of these books, I have few free coupons, mail me at valueadd2life@gmail.com.   If available, I would mail you the same.

www.ingramcontent.com/pod-product-compliance
Lightning Source LLC
Chambersburg PA
CBHW070841070326
40690CB00009B/1642